W9-BJL-271

AND THE
MOUNTAINS
ECHOED

KHALED HOSSEINI

A LITERARY REVIEW & ANALYSIS
by
EXPERT BOOK REVIEWS

Caution: We encourage you to first order a copy of Khaled Hosseini's full book, _And the Mountains Echoed_ before you read this unofficial Book Summary & Review. This review is designed to meet all reading styles. Whether you decide to use it together with the full book or using the review after reading the full book entirely depends on what suits you.

Copyright © 2013 by Expert Book Reviews. All rights reserved worldwide. No part of this publication may be reproduced or transmitted in any form without the prior written consent of the publisher.

TABLE OF CONTENTS

OVERVIEW

This is an epic tale set in the mold of *Doctor Zhivago*, in which the lives of the characters are determined, often tragically, by great historical circumstances and events that they are powerless to control. The story tells of a little Afghan girl's unlikely journey with her family. She goes from her dirt poor, but happy, existence in Shadbagh village, to relative opulence at her stepparents' Kabul house, to Paris, and back again to her disappeared village. Even then, her journey is not over. Her trek through life spans the better part of twentieth-century Afghan history to the present time, carrying with it the lives of her family members and others touched by her or connected to her one way or another.

This is a love story of a different kind. Pari, as she is named, is loved by her older brother beyond words. When she is torn from him and her family at the tender age of three, the stage is set for the suspense that will last as long as the story: will they ever meet again?

Intertwined with Pari's tale is that of her extraordinarily beautiful stepmother, Nilda, who is half-French, half-Afghan. An accomplished poet, her unfortunate circumstances lead her on a desperate quest. We also meet Pari's step-uncle, Nabi, who is responsible for setting in motion the chain of events that will determine Pari's life.

Toward the end, we meet Pari's niece (also

named Pari, in her honor), daughter of her

long-lost brother Abdullah. In between, other

characters not only flesh out Pari's

experiences, but also highlight the themes

and motifs of the story.

About The Author of *And the Mountains Echoed*

"Khaled Hosseini was born in Kabul,

Afghanistan, and moved to the United States

in 1980. His first novel, The Kite Runner,

was an international bestseller, published in

thirty-eight countries. In 2006 he was

named a goodwill envoy to UNHCR, the

United Nations Refugee Agency. He lives in

northern California." (Amazon.com)

THEMES AND MOTIFS

One of the most enduring motifs in the novel is aging, and aging's fatalistic stalker, sickness. It is not enough that aging disfigures faces and bodies. It brings along with it degenerative conditions that oftentimes rob those afflicted of what dignity they have left. The body becomes increasingly incapacitated; unable to move, the subject becomes ever more dependent, a burden to others, and most of all, to oneself. Or the mind may be lost in a haze, a fog that increasingly becomes thicker, and from which there is no return. Suleiman Wahdati, Pari Wahdati and Odelia suffer from such degenerative physical sicknesses in their old age, as does Sultana, Pari the younger's mother, while Abdullah is afflicted with dementia.

Another theme is the essential selflessness of love. We see it first in Abdullah's caring for his sister Pari, in his doing all of the difficult and unpleasant things a mother would do for a child, without being obligated to do so. We see it with Amra Adamovic's fighting for Roshi's cure against all odds. Most of all, we see it in Pari the younger's caring, first for her mother and then for her father, even though it means sacrificing her ambitions and future prospects. We even see it in Nila, flawed as she and her love for Pari may be, when she insists on staying beside

Pari as Pari lies in a hospital bed with
pneumonia.

SYMBOLS

One of the clearest and most explicit
symbols in the novel is the giant oak tree in
the village of Shadbagh. It stands for many
things. It is a symbol for the strength and
endurance of family, of community, and
even, finally, for Afghanistan itself. All of
these are shattered in one way or another,
mimicking or mirroring the mighty oak's own
demise. The fact that it is cut by the very
same person who shatters his family by
selling Pari and Pari's father, Abdullah,
underscores its meaning. The community is
later wiped out by the wars that befall

Afghanistan, while Afghanistan itself is cut down and its people uprooted by them.

Another symbol that nicely appears in the beginning of the story and again at the very end is the box full of feathers that Pari loved so much, and that Abdullah worked so hard to get. Throughout the convoluted journey on which Abdullah takes them, from a small village in Afghanistan to halfway around the world to the U.S., and then finally to France and to Pari Wahdati's hands, the box is symbolic of Abdullah's love for Pari, always with him, always present, until the feathers finally reach their intended destination. Pari's joy at receiving them becomes more poignant still by the fact that she doesn't remember them, drawing a parallel to

Abdullah's inability to remember Pari, his beloved sister, even when she is in front of him.

CONTEXT AND SETTING

As befits an epic on a grand scale, Afghanistan is at once an exotic, turbulent, enchanted and damned setting for much of the story. It gives the saga of a family a tragic and at the same time hopeful context: tragic, in its illumination of the hard choices forced on people living in a poor and oppressive culture in mid-twentieth century Afghanistan, an ancient, yet deeply patriarchal and reactionary society, but hopeful, because even though it is a reactionary society, the story shows the resilience of its people, their pride, and their dignity, which shine through, even though their land is ruined and laid to waste by its wars, whether caused by outsiders or its own bloodthirsty war lords.

The setting startles us by shifting to lands of overflowing material wealth, liberty and opportunity, especially for women, things of which Afghans could never dream in their own country (specifically, France, and the U.S.). And yet, with all the advantages and freedoms suddenly available to those who escape Afghanistan, their past lives in that country keep a hold over them that is fatal to some, but in the end, liberating to others.

CHARACTER LIST

- Pari Wahdati – main character of story; daughter of Faboor and his first wife; stepdaughter of Suleiman and Nilda Wahdati; Ph.D in mathematics

- Abdullah – Pari's older brother; his love for his kid sister underpins the whole story

- Faboor – Father of Pari and Abdullah

- Shekibh – the Mullah of Shadbagh, Pari's village

- Parwana – second wife of Faboor, stepmother of Pari and Abdullah

- Masooma – Parwana's beautiful sister who becomes disabled, and is left to die in the desert, according to her own wishes

- Nabi – Parwana's brother; chauffeur and cook of the Wahdati's; secretly in love with Mrs. Wahdati, he suggested she buy Pari

- Iqbal – Faboor's and Parwana's son; killed when trying to reclaim their lot in the village of Shadbagh

- Nila Wahdati – daughter of Afghan grandee and French mother; can't have children, due to a hysterectomy; poet; takes Pari to Paris; commits suicide

- Suleiman Wahdati – rich Afghan; homosexual in love with Nabi, possibly marries Nila for the sake of appearances

- Mr. Markos Varvaris – Greek plastic surgeon, volunteers to go to Afghanistan when Taliban is driven out; nexus between Pari's past and present

- Ms. Amra Ademovic – Bosnian nurse and aid worker, who also volunteers to go to Afghanistan; Roshi's benefactor

- Roshi – Afghan girl with traumatic head injury, adopted by Amra

- Idris – Afghan-American, a doctor , who returns to Kabul to reclaim his family's house

- Timur – Idris's brother, businessman; returns to Kabul with his brother

- Pari – American daughter of Abdullah and Sultana

- Julien – Nila Wahdati's, and later Pari Wahdati's, lover

- Colette – Pari Wahdati's childhood friend

- Eric – Pari Wahdati's husband, who dies of a heart attack in his 40s

- Isabelle – Pari Wahdati's oldest daughter

- Alain – Pari Wahdati's second child

- Thierry – Pari Wahdati's third child

- Commander Sahib – anti-Russian jihadist; lately narco-trafficker

- Adel – Commander Sahib's son

- Kabir – Commander Sahib's bodyguard

- Gholam – Iqbal's son

- Thalia – horribly disfigured childhood friend of Markos Varvaris, and companion to his mother

- Odelia – Marks' flinty and strong-willed mother, diagnosed with a wasting neurological ailment

- Madeleine – Odelia's childhood friend

- Dorian – Madeleine's first husband; owner of dog that mutilates Thalia

CHAPTER 1 SUMMARY (FALL 1952)

A father tells a bedtime story to his young

daughter, Pari and young son Abdullah. He

will leave the next day with his daughter,

leaving the boy and the mother behind.

A farmer in a small village has five children,

the youngest of which, a three-year-old boy,

is his favorite. Even though the village sits

on a too-hot and arid valley, making farming

back- breaking and unrewarding work, the

farmer is happy, because he has a happy

and loving family.

A monster by the name of *Div*, who lives

very far away, every once in a long while

comes to villages to take away the son or

daughter from an unfortunate family that

has been chosen by the *Div* to make that

sacrifice; if the family does not choose which

child should be taken, all of that family's

children will be taken instead.

The *Div* chooses the farmer's house, and he

blindly picks out from among five rocks the

one that represents his favorite son, forcing

him to give up the boy to the *Div*.

The farmer cannot live with his grief, so he

travels to the *Div's* castle to kill the monster

and take back his son, or die in the attempt.

The *Div* takes pity on him and shows him

that his son in a terrestrial paradise, where

he plays and learns and thrives. The *Div*

asks him to choose to bring him back to his village, where a drought has worsened conditions to the point at which children are dying, or leave him to enjoy the best that life can offer. The farmer decides to leave him.

Before the farmer goes back to his village, the *Div* gives him a potion to drink while going home. When he returns to his home, he has forgotten everything about his journey, including that he ever had his son. That is how the *Div* rewards the farmer for his courage and love for his son: by erasing the pain of losing him.

After his return, the drought gives way to plentiful rains and he and his family prosper; his children get married and have children.

18

In his old age, he enjoys the pleasure of a

plentiful and adoring family.

CHAPTER 2 SUMMARY (FALL 1952)

Saboor is a hard and strong man. Abdullah and Pari are his children. Saboor hits Abdullah when he insists on following his father and sister on their trip to Kabul, but in the end, relents and lets him come along. Saboor pulls a wagon with Pari and sometimes Abdullah in it on the desert road.

Abdullah's and Pari's mother has been dead for three years, and now he and his sister live with Parwana, their stepmother, and Iqbal, their half-brother. Abdullah misses his mother terribly, but understands that Parwana could never love him and his sister the way she loves Iqbal.

Pari has inherited her mother's inborn happiness and goodness. Abdullah adores her to the point of trading his only pair of shoes for a peacock's feather to give to her, as she collects feathers.

Saboor works at odd jobs: picking apples, making bricks, even building roads. His brother-in- law, Nabi, gets him a construction job in Kabul.

Abdullah believes his father blames himself for the death of his and Parwana's first child two winters ago; if he had gotten a better paying job, or more jobs, he could have provided more blankets, or even a heater.

The small party stops to rest for the night. Pari can't convince her father to tell them a story. Abdullah thinks that his father is never more alive than when he tells his stories.

Abdullah wakes up to find his father gone. As fear begins to overwhelm him, he cries out for his father in vain. At last, his father appears. Abdullah begs him not to leave them.

The next day, they reach Kabul, where step-uncle Nabi is waiting for them. Abdullah and Pari gawk at the sights and sounds as Nabi drives them to his employer's house.

Upon reaching the house, they meet Mr. and Mrs. Wahdati, Nabi's employers. Abdullah finds the house overwhelmingly large and luxurious.

Saboor and his children are introduced to the Wahdatis. Mrs. Wahdati is condescending and her husband is distant. Abdullah remembers her from a visit to Shadbagh –– she had wanted to meet Nabi's relatives. At the time, Parwana had almost died of shame from their poverty. Mrs. Wahdati offers to take Saboor's children, while Suleiman, her husband, shows Saboor the work site. Saboor assents.

The party reaches the bazaar, where Mrs. Wahdati buys Pari brand new shoes. Abdullah realizes that she means to keep Pari, begs her not to do it, and begins to cry.

She tells Abdullah that it is all for the best and that he'll understand some day.

Back in Shadbagh, Pari's absence weighs heavily on Saboor, but most of all on Abdullah, and a pall hangs over the entire household. Parwana tries to explain why Pari had to be the one to stay.

A giant oak tree that had stood for generations is cut down for firewood for the village in anticipation of the worst part of winter. Later that day, Saboor and Abdullah go to celebrate the birth of the Sheikh's son.

Abdullah finds a feather, an unbearably painful reminder of Pari. He resolves to leave the village once spring comes.

24

CHAPTER 3 SUMMARY (SPRING 1949)

Parwana's sister Masooma, who is disabled, messes her bed. Parwana stifles her despair and cleans her up, thinking that this was what she deserves.

Parwana desperately desires Saboor, but does not dare act on it. He has recently lost his wife, and is burdened with grief. She learns that he is looking for a wife.

Masooma asks Parwana if she can sleep by her side, to which she complies. They share fond memories until Masooma falls asleep. Parwana suddenly panics at the thought of her sister being her Siamese twin.

From birth, Masooma was a tranquil, popular and trouble-free child, while her twin, Parwana, the opposite.

When the girls were nine, Parwana developed a crush on Saboor. She stole a notebook to give to him, so that he could write the stories he made up, but her sister found it and gave it to him, not knowing it was hers. Parwana was crushed at the time.

When the girls reach the age of eleven, boys throw a stone at them. Attached is both a written love message and an insulting one. Masooma assumes, correctly, that the former is for her and the latter is for her sister. Parwana is deeply hurt, not so much

26

by the insult, but by her realization that her sister shares the boys' view of her.

Nabi is the success story of Parwana's family, having gotten a job in the big city. He goes back to Shadbagh every month to see her sisters, and gives Parwana money each time.

Nabi relates to Parwana Saboor had expressly told him that he was looking for a wife, but what good would it do her, when she was tied to the care of her sister for life?

When they were thirteen and the sisters went to bazaars, men's eyes were riveted on Masooma; she was an extraordinary beauty. Parwana was not, a fact of which she was

27

reminded every time she saw a man's eyes on her sister.

While smoking a hookah, Masooma tells Parwana that she wants to go to Kabul and visit Nabi. When Parwana objects out of concern for her condition, Masooma says that she got Mullah Shekib to lend them his mule.

When the sisters were seventeen, sitting high up in a branch of the old oak tree, Masooma confided to Parwana that Saboor would marry her. Parwana's pain was so great that she unconsciously arranged to have her sister fall, even as she tried to save her; Masooma was disabled as a result.

On the way to Kabul, Masooma's intention is revealed: she wants her sister to leave her to die. She tells Parwana that she no longer has a life worthy of the family name and that she, Parwana, will also be liberated by her death. Parwana is torn. On one hand, she has the chance to be free of the burden of her disabled sister, the same sister whom she had always resented to the point of hatred because she was so beautiful and beloved, while Parwana was not; on the other, she remembers the happy times they shared as children. But leaving her to die seems too much for her. In the end, she respects her sister's wish, and leaves her to die, smoking a hookah filled with opium.

CHAPTER 4 SUMMARY

Nabi begins a long letter to a Mr. Markos. At the time of its writing, he is in his mid-eighties. The letter is to be opened only after his death, and is partly meant as a confession of sorts. It is also intended for someone not yet mentioned.

The letter goes on to recount the way Nabil ended up in Kabul, at the service of Mr. Wahdati, as cook and chauffeur. To Nabi, Mr. Wahdati's life has always seemed aimless and purposeless. He has always seemed to be someone who was merely content to live off of his inheritance.

One day, Mr. Wahdati asks Nabi to drive to an exclusive neighborhood, where he goes calling on the future Mrs. Wahdati. A few days afterward, the marriage takes place in a simple ceremony.

Meanwhile Nabi learns from one of the help about the beautiful Mrs. Wahdati's compromised reputation.

The marriage is not a happy one. Meanwhile, Nabi worships Mrs. Wahdati from afar. The first time they have a conversation, Nabi relates a clever anecdote about his village that makes her laugh; Nabi is beside himself with joy at having entertained Mrs. Wahdati, or Nila, as he likes to think of her.

Nila starts to have ever more frequent conversations with Nabi. One day she asks him to take her to meet his family.

At Shadbagh, he meets Saboor's family and is enchanted by Pari. On the way back, she starts crying, confessing to Nabi that she can't have children because she had a hysterectomy.

Nila is disconsolate for a while. A visit from her father and a party, at which she reads her poems, lifts her spirits. Her last poem essentially tells the story of Saboor and Parwana; Nabi, who has been waiting on guests, feels vaguely betrayed by it.

Nila has an affair and makes Nabi complicit.
He feels somehow cuckolded, but
nevertheless, his devotion towards her
remains undiminished.

Nabi justifies his idea to have Saboor sell his
daughter to Nila by citing Nila's inability to
have a child, Saboor's family's acute need
for income, the forecast for an exceptionally
cruel winter, and the idea that in the end, it
is better for all concerned to give Nila
something no other man can. The parting
between Pari and Abdullah is as heartrending
as Nabi had foreseen.

Pari has the effect of making a family out of
the Wahdatis, even winning Mr. Wahdati's

affection, and making Nila distant from Nabi again.

Part of the agreement is that Pari's family cannot visit Pari. Nabi goes to visit them, but is told never to come again.

In 1955, as Pari turns six years old, Mr. Wahdati has a stroke that leaves him semi-paralyzed, unable to speak or walk, but able to communicate his feelings, however grotesquely. Nila is not the type of woman who can sacrifice herself to tending an invalid. She leaves for France with Pari, but not before cryptically telling Nabi as she hugs him that it was always him.

Left alone with Mr. Wahdati, Nabi finds

sketch books full of Mr. Wahdati's drawings

of him in all sorts of circumstances; he

remembers Nila's last words to him. He asks

himself, if he can stay after learning this.

Nabi does not leave. Nabi and his boss

develop a kind of intimacy. Wahdati is able

to talk again and teaches Nabi to read and

write.

Wahdati confesses that Nabi was a lousy

cook and chauffeur at first, and Wahdati

hired him only because he fell in love with

him because of his looks. He tells Nabi this

because he wants Nabi to marry before it is

too late, but Nabi already has what marriage

has to offer, except for sex, for which he

pays. Suleiman makes Nabi promise something.

In his letter, Nabi mentions the awful war years and the Taliban peace, how the house had deteriorated and been pillaged, and how he and Suleiman had become like a squabbling old couple. He took comfort from Pari's not being there, while remembering Nila and the old times as if they had been a dream.

In 2000 Nabil has to keep his promise: Suleiman has a relapse and wants to die, and Nabi has to kill him.

Suleiman leaves everything he owns to Nabi. In 2002, Nabi "rents" the house for free to a physician and aid worker who turns out to be Mr. Markos.

Nabi learns that Nila committed suicide in 1974.

After thanking Mr. Markos for his work in Afghanistan and for restoring his house, he asks him to bury him near Suleiman and to find Pari and give her the letter and his will, in which he leaves everything to her, and to tell her that he hopes that she was able to find happiness.

CHAPTER 5 SUMMARY (SPRING 2003)

Timur and Idris are cousins who left Afghanistan in the 1980s, at the start of the war and settled in California. They come back to reclaim the Bashiri family's house, which is close to the Wahdati's house. This is how they originally made Nabi's acquaintance when they were children.

Timur and Idris go to the hospital where Markos works. They've been invited by Markos after running into him earlier that day, as they looked up their house. Markos also invites them to a party at Nabi's house that night.

In the hospital, the nurse, Amra Ademovic, shows them the disfigured face of a nine-year-old girl in the hospital where she works, after they show an interest in the girl from hearing her stories.

Timur's father had sent them to Kabul, Idris's father having died nine years earlier.

Timur is the deal-maker of the family, the successful self-made businessman. He is generous, especially to Idris. Idris, who, when he had gotten married, was an intern in a hospital, needs money, but resents the way Timur advertises his generosity.

Timur and Idris are reacquainted with Nabi that night at the party. Timur is the life of the party, while Idris is ill at ease.

Idris goes out on the veranda and is joined by Amra. Amra tells Idris that she sees through Timur, and he agrees.

Amra tells Idris the story of Roshi, the nine-year-old girl. Her father's property was claimed by his older brother by tradition, but the property had been given to the younger brother because he was his father's favorite. The girl's uncle told her father he was willing to forget his claim, whereupon the girl's father invited him to a lavish dinner to celebrate their reconciliation. After dinner, the uncle excused himself to go to the outhouse. He returned with an axe and proceeded to kill the father, the mother and their two daughters and son. Roshi survived with a broken skull, from which part of her brain protruded.

Idris buys a small TV, a CD player and four movies for Roshi. He goes to the hospital where he finds Amra and the girl's uncle from her mother's side of the family. He watches a movie with Roshi until the lights go out. As he's leaving, the uncle manages to wangle money from him.

Idris visits Roshi every day and grows attached to her, but has to leave soon. Amra asks him, "What now?" He resolves to get her the surgery she needs back home. Idris

feels exhilarated at the thought.

On the plane home, Timur tells Idris he has

to go back to follow up on their effort to get

their home back, musing on the many

tragedies left behind.

Idris suffers from culture shock upon

returning and feels somewhat disconnected

with his family. His material opulence

compared to the Afghans' doesn't mean to

him what it did before.

He receives an email from Amra, who asks

about the surgery, with a note from Roshi.

He answers that he will talk to the head of

the department, and tells Roshi that his

family is eagerly awaiting her, when they don't even know she exists.

In an extraordinarily hectic and stress-filled week, Idris finds himself ashamed at feeling irritated by Amra's emails asking about the surgery.

Idris finally talks to her boss and somehow feels relieved by her negative response to his request.

Idris begins to think he judged himself too harshly, finds new comfort in his family and material well-being, and decides that his promise to Amra and Roshi was a mistake.

Six years go by. Timur pays for Roshi's surgery and she co-authors a book. Idris goes to the book signing to apologize, but is filled with shame, especially when he finds that Roshi has written on the title page, "Don't worry. You're not in it."

CHAPTER 6 SUMMARY (FEBRUARY 1974)

Nina and Pari have lived in Paris since 1955.
In 1963, when Pari is 14, they meet Julien,
an economics professor, by chance in the
emergency room, where Pari had gone after
spraining an ankle. He asks them out and
Nila, as is her wont, seduces him, but not
before he and Pari develop a secret
attraction for each other.

As is usually the case with Nila and men, she
and Julien have an intense, but ultimately
failed, romance. Meanwhile Pari fantasizes
about Julien.

Pari has not been told she is adopted and feels a strange longing for something that she has missed since childhood.

Ten years later, Pari studies mathematics and lives with her friend Colette, but no longer wants to. Pari reluctantly accompanies her to a student protest against the hunting of seals.

As they march, Julien spots and rescues Pari by inviting her to have coffee. The strong attraction they shared has survived. Pari tells him that Nila drinks too much, doesn't want to take her medication, and is about to lose her bookstore.

Shortly afterward, they move in together. Nila is angry and hurt.

Sometime after, Julien and Pari are about to go out with friends for dinner, when Nila has another drink-related accident in her apartment. Pari gets a message, picks up her mother from the hospital and takes her back to her apartment to find it in a state of extreme squalor; suddenly Pari finds her mother old, thin and frail. She resents that Julien goes out anyway.

Soon after her accident, Nila is interviewed by a poetry magazine. In the interview, she reveals her past: Her French grandfather went to Afghanistan with his daughter in 1927 to advise the king and her mother married a Pashtun aristocrat soon after. Her mother left when she was ten and died in Paris during the war. Consequently, she grew up to be rebellious and promiscuous, and her father punished her for it. She grew sick and had to be taken to India. When she came back, she felt totally lost, so she consented to marry Suleiman Wahdati. She doesn't reveal Pari's provenance, and tells her interviewer that Pari's father died of a stroke in 1955, after which she says she left for France for Pari's sake; she did everything for her sake.

Nila says she wrote poetry so as not to drown. She thinks her early poems are immature and is not proud of them. The interviewer thinks they are stunning in their capacity to elicit the exhilaration of early love, the pain of loneliness and the struggle against oppression. They are also an expression of a woman's right to define herself and her place in society – revolutionary in a society such as Afghanistan's. She ends the interview by saying that she thinks Pari is her punishment.

Soon after the interview, she commits suicide.

In 1975, Pari is overwhelmed by guilt, thinking that her affair with Julien was the final push for her mother. Pari had left Julien nine months earlier. Only now does she read the interview, realizing that it is less than truthful, but she doesn't know to what extent; this makes her feel lost, as if she suddenly doesn't know where she came from.

Desolate, she decides to get close to Colette again, so as to convince her to go to Afghanistan with her.

Pari meets Eric through Colette, and ends up marrying him. As they are about to go to Afghanistan, she finds out she is pregnant with her first child, and decides against going. She no longer feels the urgent need for answers, even though the questions are still there; she fills grounded and fulfilled now with her family. She earns her PhD in mathematics and becomes a successful academic. They settle down and have three children: Isabelle, Alain and Thierry.

In a hotel room, after giving a lecture in Munich, Eric calls her at 2:30 a.m., telling her that he thinks Isabelle has leukemia. She thinks she won't be able to cope. After calling Colette's husband, a psychiatry student, and learning from him that it is probably nothing more than a cold sore, she realizes what her mother felt, and feels an unexpected kinship.

On vacation in 1994, Pari catches herself in the mirror and realizes that at 44, she is no longer young, her looks gone. The next year, her husband has a heart attack and dies of another one three years later.

By 2010, Pari lives in a one-bedroom apartment, alone. The rheumatism that afflicts her has forced her into early retirement. Her daughter Isabelle, with three children, lives nearby, and her son Alain lives in Madrid with four. Her son Thierry is eastern Chad; he only communicates through Isabelle.

Markos has contacted her through Facebook and told her to expect his call. She no longer is sure that she wants to know about her past; her present, comprised of her extended family, career, and Colette, is a true blessing.

Nevertheless, she listens as Markos reads the letter, and memories of her childhood come rushing back, even the memories of her brother; now she understands what the gaping hole in her life had been. She resolves to go to Afghanistan.

CHAPTER 7 SUMMARY (SUMMER 2009)

Baba jan inaugurates a school for girls in

Shadbagh-e-nau, "Shadbagh the new," as

his young son, Adel, proudly looks on. Baba

jan is the benefactor of the town, having

donated a hospital, given small loans and so

forth to the townspeople. He is known as

"Commander Sahib," thanks to the time that

he fought the Russians.

Map of Afghanistan. Image Courtesy of CC

Baba jan, his son and his bodyguard, Kabir, drive back home. Their house is a fortified compound in Shadbagh-e-Kohna, "Shadbagh the old." Baba jan tells Adel he must go away to oversee his cotton fields and factory in Helmand. Adel is very sad, but understands.

Later that day, Adel witnesses a scene between a man and a boy who had tried to approach his father earlier in the school ceremony. Kabir turns them away.

Adel and his mother spend most of their time in the compound for security reasons, resulting in Adel being terribly bored. Adel goes out of the house to play with a soccer ball by his father's orchards. There, he runs into the boy he saw before. Adel challenges him to a couple of shootouts, which he wins.

As they rest, Gholam tells Adel that he was born in a refugee camp in Pakistan, where he and his brothers were raised by his father, Iqbal, and his grandmother Parwana. When Pakistan closed the refugee camp, he and his father had returned to the deserted Shadbagh-e-Kohna.

Adel tells Gholam that his father is away tending his cotton fields; this confession seems to amuse Gholam. He challenges Adel to another shootout, on the condition that if he wins, Adel will give him his favorite

Zidane t-shirt. Gholam wins handily, and leaves Adel almost crying.

After several days, Gholam comes back and gives the Zidane t-shirt back to Adel; he had sold it, and then taken it back forcibly from the boy to whom he sold it.

Gholam tells Adel his grandfather chopped down the oak tree by the side of the orchards; he had the right to do so, because it was in his property. He goes on to tell Adel that Baba-jan appropriated Gholam's family's land, bulldozed his father's house, and built the compound and orchards there.

Adel reacts with shame and anger. In response, Gholam asks him to ask his father what, in reality, he has growing in Helmand.

Adel rationalizes what he has just learned. Didn't his father say that people said bad things about him just because they were jealous? Hadn't he donated money for schools and given out loans?

When they meet again, Adel hands Gholam a coat. Gholam tells him that the Kabul judge said that Markos Varvaris' papers proving ownership of the property were burnt in an accident; the judge had been bribed with a gold watch.

At a dinner party, stones come crashing into the house. Adel just manages to spot the old man at the front porch with rocks in his hands. His father and bodyguards step out, Kabir with a steel truncheon. Adel later finds the old man's bloodied, broken glasses in the orchids.

Adel begins to realize the monstrosity of his life, the fear people have of his father, and his real activities in Helmand. Then he begins to reconcile this traumatizing new knowledge with the realization that there is nothing he can do about it.

CHAPTER 8 SUMMARY (FALL 2010)

Markos' mother, a flinty, strong-willed school teacher, by now retired, was widowed right after his birth. She had become estranged from her best friend, Madeleine. After fifteen years, she wants to visit her friend, along with her daughter, Thalia.

Thalia wears a mask because she was bitten by a dog. When Markos, who is 12, sees her face without the mask, he drops a tray with tea and pastries and starts retching. When her mother arrives at the scene and sees Thalia, a tear rolls from her eye.

Thalia leaves Markos, who is in Kabul, a phone message to call his mother.

Markos reluctantly calls her mother. His mother wants to know about Pari. Pari was moved almost to tears by the memories the house conjured. She wanted to go to Shadbagh. She only took personal possessions and allowed Markos to stay, rent-free.

Markos's mother is diagnosed with a degenerative nervous system disease; Thalia takes care of her.

Markos recoils from having to share his house, and especially the dinner table, with Thalia. She drips food all over the place and makes strange noises when she eats.

Her mother is quite lively, and takes up all the conversations. She complains about the brutality of men -- first her father's, then her first husband's. It turns out that Thalia and Odelia, Markos's mother, are kindred spirits, Thalia being an unusually bright girl.

Odie forces Markos to go to the beach with Thalia. There, she tells Markos she doesn't like it any more than he does.

Markos diagnoses Odie's strategy: to hold people obligated to her after she does something exceptional for them. In that way, she compromises the virtue of her acts. They then disappoint Odie, including Markos, so she feels grimly superior to them, which is why Markos put thousands of miles between

them for the better part of thirty years. She

does this, Markos thinks, out of insecurity

and fear.

From then on, Markos and Thalia are

expected to be on their own, wandering

around the island of Tinos, where they live.

In one such excursion, Markos looks

longingly at a camera on display; he wants

to be a photographer. Thalia knows this and

asks him why he doesn't have a camera.

Then she asks if he has a box at home.

As Madeleine is telling Odie her life story

downstairs, Thalia is making a camera out of

a shoebox. Because of her tone of voice,

Markos thinks Madeleine seeks Odie's

sympathy and consolation. Odie is not good at it. She thinks grief is private, and has never cried, herself.

Thalia tells Markos that tomorrow, he will take the first picture of his career.

They go down to the beach to take a picture. Markos wants Thalia to be in it, but she only consents if her face doesn't show; the picture is of her backside and head.

Thalia's stepfather leaves her an inheritance and she, in turn, gives half of it to Markos. He travels all over the world, taking pictures, mailing the copies to Thalia; throughout, he keeps that first picture of Thalia at the beach.

In India, he catches hepatitis and almost dies. At the hospital, he lies next to a boy who is dying of a tumor. Markos decides to volunteer once he recovers, and takes care of the boy. After wandering aimlessly for another year, he decides to apply to medical school, inspired by the boy's anguish.

Thalia confides to Markos that Madeleine has a lover, a director, with whom she will shoot in the fall. She is going to leave her present husband and leave Tinos and Thalia behind for a while.

Thalia tells Markos she is the product of a one-night stand. Her first stepfather, Dorian, was a drunk, who had a mean dog. The dog bit her, and the subsequent operation was botched, disfiguring her even more.

After Madeline leaves, Odie told Thalia she doesn't have to wear her mask. Odie tries but can't home-school Thalia and Markos, because villagers and especially children, cannot be kept away. They are always trying to catch a glimpse of Thalia. Odie resolves to take Thalia to school without the mask. People recoil, but from that point, she never wears a mask again.

With time Thalia is accepted in Tinos. Her mother elopes with the director, leaving Thalia. She receives a letter from her stepfather, offering to pay her way in a private school in London.

Thalia asks Markos for advice. He tells her that, even though he would miss her, she should study at university and become a researcher or inventor. Thalia tells Markos she could not. To Odie's well-hidden relief, she decides to stay.

Markos decides to become a plastic surgeon to right the injustice, at least a little bit, of outward appearances that could condemn someone to a life of unfulfilled potential, as in Thalia's case. But he also recognizes that he is in it for the money and prestige. He spends half of his time in Athens making money, and the other half traveling abroad to operate on people who can't afford his services.

More than thirty years later, in 2002, Markos finds Madeleine's obituary. She had founded a successful theater company. Markos resents her success, thinking she should have had a tragic life and death as retribution for leaving Thalia. But then he recognizes himself in her, too, her desire to escape, to cut off the anchors that tied her down.

Amra Ademovic, with whom he once had a fling, contacts him to tell him they need a plastic surgeon in Kabul; he decides to go for three months and winds up staying indefinitely.

In the fall of 2010, Markos goes back to visit her mother and Thalia. His mother is in her mid-fifties now; her hair is all white, reminding him of his own aging.

Though she doesn't need to, she works as an IT technician; before, she had been an appliance technician, always self-taught.

Markos hasn't been home in decades. He tiptoes into Odie's bedroom. She's asleep. He has difficulty reconciling his memories of her with her present old and sick state.

Thalia tells him his mother tries to find out everything about him on the internet. The digital pictures he sent are in a picture frame in her bedroom.

Thalia still refuses after all this time to have him fix her disfigured face. She tells him it's who she is.

Odie comes down and greets Markos. She worries about his being in a dangerous place. He, in turn, worries about her deteriorating health. In the end she tells him something he never expected to hear, namely that he turned out well.

The next day, there is a solar eclipse. As they watch the eclipse and the sickle-shaped light on Odie's hands, a magical moment occurs. With Markos holding his mother's hand in his own; he feels he has bridged the gigantic chasm between them.

CHAPTER 9 SUMMARY (WINTER 2010)

Abdullah meets his future wife in Pakistan when they are forty. They have an only child, whom they name Pari. When their Pari is small, she fantasizes that the original Pari is her twin sister.

Growing up, young Pari struggles between her Muslim upbringing and her identity as an American girl. She has to take Farsi classes and go to the Mosque, where she is told the innumerable things she has to avoid.

She helps her parents in their Afghan restaurant, and likes it as a child, but not as a teen-ager.

She earns a scholarship to a good arts college; she is beside herself with joy. Her father is devastated with sorrow at letting her go.

Just before she is to leave for college, her mother is diagnosed with cancer. She stays.

Pari often takes her sick mother on short trips. On their last trip, Pari's mother tells her that her father has a half-brother in a refugee camp in Pakistan, with family to whom he sends money. She also tells Pari it won't be long before she dies, and how good and strong God has made her; this is Pari's fondest and strongest memory of her mother.

Now Pari takes care of her father, who is well on his way to losing his mind, desperately asking for his wife, who had died earlier. Pari had taken care of her when she was dying, and now does the same for her father, sacrificing any plans she might have had for herself. Hector is a neighbor and disabled ex-marine who served in Afghanistan. He is a good friend and helps her take care of her father. They talk over the phone as she races to the airport to pick up someone.

Pari is going to pick up her older namesake. Pari the elder is overtaken with joy when they meet. As they are about to reach Pari the younger's house, the elder Pari is suddenly filled with anxiety at meeting her long-lost brother.

Abdullah is watching TV, and is impatient as his daughter shuts the sound off and introduces Pari; Abdullah doesn't react to seeing his long-lost sister. Pari talks to her brother, but his daughter can tell his mind is somewhere else.

Pari asks if he knows why he named his daughter Pari, but he does not. Through the haze of his deteriorated brain and memories, he manages to hum the tune that goes with a rhyme that Pari partly remembers, and he manages to recite the part she doesn't remember. She is overjoyed and convinced, momentarily, that she has broken through the haze, but his daughter knows better, and soon she will, too.

Abdullah falls asleep. Pari remembers when her namesake aunt first called, how incredible and at the same time how foreordained it had been. Her aunt had traveled to Shadbagh and found the narco-mansion, taking the place where she and his brothers had been born. A friend of Iqbal's had told her Abdullah's whereabouts, and she managed to reach Pari.

As they share a cup of coffee, Pari shares her life, showing a photo album full of pictures of her children and her mother; she regrets not having been kinder to her mother, like the other Pari.

Pari stays for a month. In a park Pari asks her brother if he remembers he had a sister, at which Abdullah begins weeping uncontrollably. A week later, she tells him she is his sister, driving him into a fit of rage that his daughter manages to control.

Right after he falls asleep, his daughter shows Pari the postcards she had written to her -- that is, to her imagined sister. With this revelation, they each become whole in the realization of the significance of the other's existence.

Pari goes to visit her aunt Pari in Paris, but before doing so, she applies to the college of Arts and Sciences at San Francisco State.

From Paris they go to Avignon, where there will be a great family reunion, with all of Pari's children and grandchildren in attendance, including Thierry.

Pari has left Abdullah in a nursing home. He has suffered a stroke and can no longer speak. Contrary to her expectations, the nursing home is much better than she supposed. She leaves for two weeks, the longest that she has ever been away from her father.

Before leaving for Paris Pari finds a box with an envelope taped to it, addressed to Pari, his sister, in Abdullah's handwriting. The letter, read to her aunt by Pari, says that he hopes his sister will find the box, so she'll know how he feels before his disease robs

him of his mind, as he had written it just

after his diagnosis. The tin box contains the

feathers Pari had so loved as a child, and for

which Abdullah had sacrificed so much for

her pleasure. Pari is overwhelmed with

emotion and weeps, even though she doesn't

remember the feathers, but they are

reminders of how much he loved and

remembered her until the end.

The two Paris are side by side, with one

weeping and holding the tin box. That night

at the hotel, Pari watches her aunt as she

sleeps. She rejoices at the thought of

meeting Pari's family, her flesh and blood;

she is not alone. She marvels at her aunt's

resemblance to Abdullah. She touches the elder Pari's brow as she falls asleep.

Brother and sister are children again. They are in an idyllic country setting. She falls asleep on her brother as she feels herself engulfed in absolute calm, untroubled and radiant.

ANALYSIS

No amount of factual history can give as deep and vivid a sense of the reality of Afghanistan in the last seventy years as this story gives. Likewise, no mere reporting or film documentary can give as lucid an account of the cruel decisions forced on people living on the verge of destitution, of the nuances and characteristics of such an ancient, hide-bound, complex and reactionary, but proud country as Afghanistan. It's no wonder that empires, past and present, floundered in their attempts to conquer her.

But Afghanistan is just the setting, the background, for a profound exploration of the human soul, its capacity for good and evil, paradoxically often at the same time and by the same person. In that way, the novel unblinkingly sheds light on the glory and the tawdriness that is human nature, dissecting it to show its varied shades of good and bad. It gives insight into the true nature of love and its nemesis, selfishness. Even then, love is not unsullied by selfishness, or selfishness necessarily condemned, but rather is sometimes portrayed as a legitimate struggle to fulfill one's destiny. In that way, the story engenders humility when it comes to judging any person's motives and actions, making it

more difficult to condemn or exalt in a
reflexive manner.

In human affairs, there are few, if any,
absolutes. The one perfect and true love
portrayed is that between children, and even
that is cut short. Had it not been truncated
maybe it too, would have survived, intact or
not, thanks to the interplay between
treacherous human nature, inexorable
circumstance and the relentless passage of
time.

Readers Who Enjoyed This Ebook Might Also Enjoy...

Khaled Hosseini's *And the Mountains Echoed* (the full book)

M. L. Stedman's *The Light Between Oceans*

Jeannette Walls's *The Silver Star*

Khaled Hosseini's *The Kite Runner*

Limit of Liability/Disclaimer of Warranty: The publisher and author make no representations or warranties with respect to the accuracy or completeness of these contents and disclaim all warranties such as warranties of fitness for a particular purpose. The author or publisher are not liable for any damages whatsoever. The fact that an individual or organization is referred to in this document as a citation or source of information does not imply that the author or publisher endorses the information that the individual or organization provided. This concise summary is unofficial and is not authorized, approved, licensed, or endorsed by the original book's author or publisher.

30072228R00050

Made in the USA
Lexington, KY
17 February 2014